IN THE PAST

Seaside Holidays

Dereen Taylor

WAYLAND

Explore the world with **Popcorn** - your complete first non-fiction library.

Look out for more titles in the **Popcorn** range. All books have the same format of simple text and striking images. Text is carefully matched to the pictures to help readers to identify and understand key vocabulary.
www.waylandbooks.co.uk/popcorn

First published in 2009 by Wayland

Copyright © Wayland 2009

Wayland
Hachette Children's Books
338 Euston Road
London NW1 3BH

Wayland Australia
Level 17/207 Kent Street
Sydney NSW 2000

Editor: Julia Adams
Designer: Alix Wood
Picture Researcher: Diana Morris

British Library Cataloguing in Publication Data:
Taylor, Dereen
   Seaside holidays. - (Popcorn. In the past)
   1. Seaside resorts - History - Juvenile literature
   2. Vacations - History - Juvenile literature
   I. Title
   394.2'69146'09

ISBN 978 0 7502 5781 7

Printed and bound in China

Wayland is a division of Hachette Children's Books,
an Hachette UK Company.
www.hachette.co.uk

Acknowledgements:
Alex Dellow/Hulton Archive/Getty Images: front cover, 11. English Heritage/HIP/Topfoto: 10. Harry Kerr/Hulton Archive/Getty Images: 13. Jose Luis Pelaez/Blend Images/Corbis: 23. Picturepoint/Topfoto: 2, 14, 15. Paul Popper/Popperfoto/Getty Images: 16, 19. The Print Collector/HIP/Topfoto: 20. Rolf Richardson/Alamy: 7. Stone/Getty Images: 21. Three Lions/Hulton Archive/Getty Images: 9. Topfoto: 1, 4, 5, 6, 8, 17, 18. Ullstein Bild/Topfoto: 12. Andy Crawford: 23

☀ **Contents**

Holiday time

In the past, holidays at the beach were very popular. Rich Victorian families went away for two weeks or more each summer.

In Victorian times, people wore long clothes to the beach. They never wore swimming costumes.

Every year, poor families had
just one day out by the sea.

Some beaches got very crowded
in the summer!

By the sea

In the 1900s, seaside resorts became very popular. They had a promenade to walk along and a pier built out into the sea.

Families wore their best clothes to walk along this promenade in Scarborough.

1891

Many piers are still enjoyed today, more than 100 years after they were built. A lot of piers have theatres and shops on them, too.

Eastbourne pier was built in 1872.
You can still visit it today!

On the beach

In the 1900s, people thought their bodies should always be covered. That is why children wore lots of clothes on the beach, even if it was very hot.

These Victorian children were allowed to roll up their trousers and skirts when they were playing by the sea.

In the 1950s, children wore swimming costumes and trunks. They were made of thick cotton.

Ask your parents and grandparents what they wore on the beach when they were children.

Eating candy floss on the beach was a special treat in the 1950s.

Lots to do

The seaside was a great place to see and do different things. Children could watch a Punch and Judy puppet show.

1949

This is a Punch and Judy show on Lowestoft beach.

Donkeys used to carry children up
and down the beach. You can still go
for donkey rides on some beaches today.

1955

Blackpool

Blackpool is in the north of England.
It has been one of the most popular
British seaside resorts for over 100 years.

1890s

Blackpool Tower first opened in 1894,
and it is still enjoyed by tourists today.

Blackpool had many special things for tourists to enjoy, like the electric tramline. It was the first tramline in England when it opened in 1885.

Trams were a fun way to travel along the sea front.

1956

Holiday camps

In the 1950s, holiday camps became popular. They were made up of lots of holiday homes for families. Many were close to the seaside.

This holiday camp in Minehead was so big, it even had its own shops and a post office.

1960s

Holiday camps had fun activities, too.
You could go cycling or roller skating.
There were even bike races and
games competitions.

1950

These children are learning how to roller skate
at a Butlins holiday camp in Skegness.

☀ Let's go camping!

In the 1960s and 1970s, families often went on holiday in a caravan. They stayed on camp sites with many other families.

Many camp sites were built close to the seaside.

1965

Some families went camping in a tent.
It was cheaper than a caravan, so
families could afford longer holidays
than in the past.

1970s

Going abroad

In the 1900s, only rich families could afford to go on holiday in a foreign country.

This family is spending their holiday on the Belgian coast, close to Oostende.

1900

In the 1960s, air travel became more affordable. Many British families started to spend their holidays abroad.

1960

Benidorm in Spain was very popular for holidays. It was sunny and had lovely sandy beaches.

Postcards and souvenirs

People sent postcards to their friends and family. They wrote about the fun things they had done at the seaside.

1928

WEST PIER AND ITALIAN GARDENS, BRIGHTON.

This postcard shows Brighton pier.

They also brought home souvenirs, to remember the special times they enjoyed while they were away.

What is your favourite holiday souvenir?

Where do you think these souvenirs come from?

Timeline

1662 The first British Punch and Judy show is performed. They become very popular in Victorian times.

1870s The first piers and promenades are built at seaside resorts.

1871 Bank holidays are introduced in the UK. This means workers now get paid on a day's holiday.

1894 The first picture postcards are sent.

1894 Blackpool Tower opens.

1936 The first Butlins holiday camp opens in Skegness, Lincolnshire.

1940s Swimming costumes and trunks become popular beachwear.

1960s Camping and caravanning holidays start to become popular with British families.

1970s Air travel becomes more affordable. More British families spend their holiday abroad. Spain is the most popular holiday destination.

Make a postcard

Make your own holiday postcard from the past!

1. Interview your grandparents and find out what they did on their favourite seaside holiday as a child. Where did they go? What did they see?

2. Take a postcard-sized piece of card. On one side, draw a picture of something special from their holiday memories.

3. Turn the card over. Use a black pen and a ruler to divide the card in half. Then draw lines for the address on one half.

4. Using the details from your grandparents' holiday, write about what you have seen and done. Then post it to them as a nice surprise!

Glossary

holiday camp   A place offering accommodation and activities for people on holiday.

pier   A platform built for walking out over the sea. Some piers have shops and amusements on them.

promenade   A path along a seafront.

resort   A place where people go on holiday.

souvenir   Something that you keep to remind you of a special person or place.

tourist   A person who visits a place on holiday.

tramline   The special track that a tram rides on.

Victorian   Belonging to the time when Queen Victoria was on the throne (1837–1901).

Index